# Change the World:

## Poems for Positive Action

By Wayne Visser

Paperback edition published in 2023

by Kaleidoscope Futures, Narborough, UK.

Cover photography and design by Wayne Visser.

Printing and distribution by Lulu.com.

978-1-908875-98-3

**Non-fiction Books by Wayne Visser**

Beyond Reasonable Greed: Why Sustainable Business is a Much Better Idea!

South Africa: Reasons to Believe

Corporate Citizenship in Africa: Lessons from the Past, Paths to the Future

Business Frontiers: Social Responsibility, Sustainable Development and Economic Justice

The A to Z of Corporate Social Responsibility: A Complete Reference Guide to Concepts, Codes and Organisations

Making A Difference: Purpose-Inspired Leadership for Corporate Sustainability & Responsibility

Landmarks for Sustainability

The Top 50 Sustainability Books

The World Guide to CSR: A Country by Country Analysis of Corporate Sustainability and Responsibility

The Age of Responsibility: CSR 2.0 and the New DNA of Business

The Quest for Sustainable Business: An Epic Journey in Search of Corporate Responsibility

Corporate Sustainability & Responsibility: An Introductory Text on CSR Theory & Practice – Past, Present & Future

CSR 2.0: Transforming Corporate Sustainability and Responsibility

Disrupting the Future: Great Ideas for Creating a Much Better World

This is Tomorrow: Artists for a Sustainable Future

Sustainable Frontiers: Unlocking Change Through Business, Leadership and Innovation

The CSR International Research Compendium: Volumes 1-3

The World Guide to Sustainable Enterprise: Volumes 1-4

The Little Book of Quotations on Social Responsibility

The Little Book of Quotations on Sustainable Business

The Little Book of Quotations on Transformational Change

Purpose Inspired: Reflections on Conscious Living: Volumes 1-5

Thriving: The Breakthrough Movement to Regenerate Nature, Society and the Economy

Everyday Inspiration: Philosophy for Daily Living

## Fiction Books by Wayne Visser

I Am An African: Favourite Africa Poems

Wishing Leaves: Favourite Nature Poems

Seize the Day: Favourite Inspirational Poems

String, Donuts, Bubbles and Me: Favourite Philosophical Poems

African Dream: Inspiring Words & Images from the Luminous Continent

Icarus: Favourite Love Poems

Life in Transit: Favourite Travel & Tribute Poems

The Poetry of Business: A CEO's Quest for Meaning

Follow Me! (I'm Lost): The Tale of an Unexpected Leader

## About the Author

Dr Wayne Visser is a globally recognised "pracademic", poet and "possibilist" on the impact of business on nature and society, with faculty roles at the University of Cambridge and Antwerp Management School. He is also director of the thinktank Kaleidoscope Futures, founder of CSR International, and former director of Sustainability Services at KPMG and strategy analyst at Capgemini. He has written 44 books, including seven previous collections of poetry, five Purpose Inspired volumes, and two works of fiction. He has travelled to 78 countries and been listed as a top 100 thought leader in trustworthy business. Dr Visser lives in Norfolk, UK.

Website: www.waynevisser.com

Email: wayne@waynevisser.com

# Contents

**Change the World**

*Part 1*

Let's change the world, let's shift it
Let's shake and remake it
Let's rearrange the pieces
The patterns in the maze
The reason for our days
In ways that make it better
In shades that make it brighter
That make the burden lighter
Because it's shared, because we dared
To dream and then to sweat it
To make our mark and not regret it
Let's plant a seed and humbly say:
I changed the world today!

Let's change the world, let's lift it

Let's take it and awake it

Let's challenge every leader

The citadels of power

The prisoners in the tower

The hour of need's upon us

It's time to raise our voices

To stand up for our choices

Because it's right, because we fight

For all that's just and fair

For a planet we can share

Let's join the cause and boldly say:

We'll change the world today!

Let's change the world, let's love it

Let's hold it and unfold it

Let's redesign the future

The fate of earth and sky

The existential why

Let's fly to where there's hope

To where the world is greener

Where air and water's cleaner

Because it's smart to make a start

To fix what we have broken

Our children's wish unspoken

Let's be the ones who rise and say:

We changed the world today!

## Nature Knows

When all the world seems upside down
The fool's on the hill
The king is a clown
When headline news loud-speaks the views
Of puppeteers of fears
And naysayers of the truth
When leaders' voices are hollow choices
Of dumb-down beats of tweets
And two-fingers to the youth
Take a step back from the black
And white, the stereotype
The media hype, the Trumptown blues
And choose a world of hues
From greens to greys, and reds to browns
The rounds of seasons, synchro-reasons
Of sun and moon, the tune
Of vitality that sprouts and grows
The harmony, the symphony, the flows
That nature knows

When all the roads seem nowhere bound

The signs contradict

The noise has no sound

When every maze just adds to the craze

Of shallow aims in games

And hamster wheels for jobs

When Wall Street belies, in suits and ties

Their ugly creed of greed

And clever ways to rob

Take a deep breath, defy the death

Of hope, the hangman's rope

The doomsday dope, the victim's shoes

And choose a forest of clues

Of roots and shoots

From seeds to stems, and buds to leaves

The trees of jungles, the rumbles

Of beast and storm, the dawn

Of light and flight and lucent bows

The illumination, the revelation, the glows

That nature shows

When all that's lost can scarce be found
The love swept away
The faith nearly drowned
When silent strings, like broken wings
Leave empty spaces in places
Where music once soared
When prophets' words sound more absurd
Than the Mad Hatter's patter
And the Jabberwocky's chord
Take a great leap, take time to reap
What you have sown, from flesh and bone
From mind clone and idea muse
And choose an earthscape of do's
Not don't's and won't's
But can's and will's, and better still
The thrills of striving, life thriving
Through trial and error, through terror
To yellow dreams and scarlet rose
The magnificence, the intelligence, the prose
That nature knows.

**Alive**

I live
And therefore, I am victorious
Every breath is a triumph
Every step, an accomplishment
For living and breathing and walking
Are acts of defiance
Against dying and resigning and stopping

I am alive
And therefore, I am miraculous
Every emotion is an improbability
Every idea, an implausible feat
For living and feeling and thinking
Are audacious abilities
Against the odds of chance and chaos

I survive

And therefore, I am heroic

Every day is a battle won

Every year, a universe conquered

For surviving and striving and thriving

Are human superpowers

Against oblivion and entropy and
  meaninglessness


We live

And while we live, others die

Every life is an arc of light

Every death, a shooting star

For living and shining and fading

Are the black fate

Of each glorious being whose life we celebrate

We are alive

And therefore, we are guardians of life

Every heartbeat is a sacred gift

Every experience, a rare treasure

For living and laughing and loving

Are anti-spells

Against dying and darkness and desolation


We survive

And therefore, we are incredible

Every sunrise is another chance

Every moonrise, another bridge

For surviving and rising and connecting

Are acts of courage

That honour creation

And welcome living

And reaffirm life.

## Next

You never know what's coming next,
around the corner, around the bend
in life's twisted maze; there are no signs,
no rules, no lines unbroken, no guarantees,
for more is spoken than is known,
more unwoken than the mind's eager eye -
the sigh of invisible breezes, blown fragments
of meaning, like leaf-piles scattered
as we chase our dreams, the things that
matter, the pitter-patter of love,
the flitter-fluttering dove of inner peace,
of calm in the maelstrom of motion,
our incessant becoming, our running
from the past and striving to be
different, better, elsewhere, anywhere
other than where we are, away
from the storm, the swarm of buzzing thoughts
and bustling tasks, yet no one asks:

what for and why now, why so urgent,

this need to strive, to plot and plan,

to map the stars and our orbit through

the spaces of living, the traces of dying,

the faces of who we are and who we will be -

until, at last, we are free, unvexed

by what, or who, is coming next.

## Children at a Funeral

The shadow moved across the sun
And turned my world a pallid grey
The tide of mourning had begun
And then I saw the children play

They did not soothe my aching grief
They did not make the burden light
But as they played, I felt relief
A candle glowing in my night

The steady rain began to fall
And washed the poison from death's sting
A sea of faces paid respect
And then I heard the children sing

They did not take my loss away
They did not turn the bitter sweet
But as they sang, I glimpsed a ray
A cycle turning, now complete

The rumbling storm brought lashing hail
Like pounding fists upon my heart
My anger rose to howling gale
And then I heard the children laugh

They did not dry my veil of tears
They did not make my dark skies blue
But as they laughed, I took a breath
And gained the strength to start anew.

## In the Game

Every day, you're in the game
You're dodging and dribbling, blocking and
    shooting
Rooting for the team, the change
From attack to defense, on the counter
From the back to the scoring zone
Your fans, your friends, your family
Are shouting your name, counting
The hoops, the scoops, the victories.

Every day, you're taking the hits
You're collecting the knocks, the bruises
From losers, when life won't play fair
You share the defeats, the repeats
The scares and the shake-downs
The days when scoring is rare
When the flare is extinguished
Yet still you bounce back, rise again.

Every day, you're playing for keeps

You're ducking and diving, weaving and
    scheming

Dreaming of making your shots, the aim

Is so crucial, grace of the movement

From eye to hand, hand to hoop

We whoop in your triumph, your successes

For win or lose, it matters not

What matters is the game, going far

And in our eyes, you're always a star.

## A Dream to be Painted

It is time to pause, to breathe, to savour
As the wheel of life spins in your favour
It's a moment to rest, to gather, to reflect
To look back, to look forward and to accept

This is your season of fruits, of growing
After long years of ploughing and sowing
It's a change in the rhythm, the motion
A new moon waxing to the sway of the ocean

It's a time of rebirth, of conceiving
From a lifetime of giving, now receiving
It's a fresh white canvass, a future untainted
New palette and brushes, a dream to be
    painted.

## Spirit of the Mountain

We climb, not because the mountain is there

But because there is great joy in climbing

We climb, not because we want to conquer the
peaks

But because we want to test our own limits

We climb, not because ascending is easy or
direct

But because it is a struggle that strengthens us


The summit is wherever we want to go

Knowing that we will have to work to get there

The summit is whatever we dream of becoming

Knowing that every step we take brings us
closer

The summit is however we envision a better
world

Knowing that all change begins with us

We rest, not because we are defeated

But because we like to savour the view

We rest, not because we are weak or soft

But because we respect the rhythms of life

We rest, not because we wish to stop

But because we plan to go on even longer


The mountain is every barrier before us

Knowing that our body can rise to the
challenge

The mountain is every opportunity ahead

Knowing that our mind is a source of great
power

The mountain is every aspiration we nurture

Knowing that our spirit is the crucible of
creation.

## Patient Dreams

I wish you all the best in life
Through seasons and extremes
But most of all I wish for you
The gift of patient dreams

I hope you'll travel far and wide
Cross oceans, mountains, streams
But also find within your mind
The land of patient dreams

I trust you'll be a great success
However hard it seems
To take your time and stone by stone
To build your patient dreams

I know you'll suffer some defeats
There'll be ill-fated schemes
And yet you'll rise and rise again
Recalling patient dreams

I wish you joy and love in life
With rainbows and sunbeams
But most of all, in great and small
I wish you patient dreams.

## Ideas

I was born in the dark
Hardly more than a spark
And it's true, I don't know
Where I'm going
But be gentle on me
Do not judge what you see
I am just an idea
But I'm growing

I don't yet have a name
Neither fortune nor fame
And it's true, I can't say
What I'm showing
But just give me some time
For my rhythm and rhyme
Will get better the longer
I'm flowing

I have things still to learn
I might speak out of turn
And it's true, I can't prove
What I'm knowing
But the wheel's now in spin
If you just count me in
I may change your whole world
And keep growing

## Tree Braille

I touch your living skin
And feel the pulse of seasons
Read the code of secrets
I tap your living mind
And hear the tangle of tales
Sense the sorrow of loss
Connect with ancient wisdom

## Nature's Embrace

Take me to the forests green
I need to feel their healing balm
To soak in groves of dappled sheen
And wallow in their soothing calm

Take me to the mountains high
I need to stretch and strain and strive
To rise up where the eagles fly
And burst with joy to be alive

Take me to the wilderness
I need the space to be alone
To tap the vein of nature's bliss
And slip into the mindful zone

Take me to the beaches gold
I need to feel the sun's warm rays
To dive into the oceans cold
And drift on lunar tidal sways

Take me to the valleys cool
I need to rest within their shade
To cast ideas into a pool
And watch them ripple 'til they fade

Take me to the desert sand
I need to clear my cluttered mind
To see the beauty in the bland
And treasure secrets that I find

Take me to the alpine snow
I need to breathe its pristine chill
To thaw my soul while embers glow
And feel the pure adrenal thrill

Take me into nature's arms
I need to feel her love embrace
To shelter from life's daily harms
And gaze upon her wizened face

## Be An Optimist

Be an optimist
Not because the future is bright
But because bright people are working
To make the future better
Be an optimist
Not because the news is good
But because good people are showing
That change is always possible
Be an optimist
Not because the world is fair
But because fair people are fighting
For justice wherever it is needed

When ordinary people do extraordinary things

Let your heart beat a little faster

Knowing that you are ordinary too

When inspiring leaders rise to our biggest
challenges

Let your sights be set a little higher

Knowing that you too can inspire

When young voices join in the call to action

Let your efforts go a little further

Knowing that you can always do more

Be an optimist

Not because the night is over

But because we all carry the light of values

And remember the promise of dawn

Be an optimist

Not because victory is certain

But because we have the opportunity

To still make a positive difference

Be an optimist

Not because the Earth is a haven

But because we have a growing desire

To be guardians for all life

When the clouds of gloom are gathering

Let your knowledge of the sun and skies above

Be a vision that brings perspective

When the drums of war are beating

Let your refusal to cast others as villains

Be a declaration of our common humanity

When the tides of bigotry are rising

Let your belief that we all have equal worth

Be a boat that will never capsize

Be an optimist

Not because you ignore the facts

But because the wider landscape of facts

Tell a story of remarkable progress

Be an optimist

Not because the glass is half full

But because we always have the chance

To tap a greater source of power

Be an optimist

Not because you are blind and deaf and dumb

But because you see and hear and speak

More clearly what is possible.

## Your Mission

Your mission
In this short, sacred life
Is to discover your voice
Your unique identity
Your way of being in the world
Your mission
Is to locate your inner core
Your centre of gravity
Your place
In a universe of diffuse chaos

Your mission

In this raw, random life

Is to discover your gift

Your unique talent

Your way of giving in the world

Your mission

Is to locate your playing-field

Your zone of impact

Your mark

In a universe of constant change

Your mission

In this cruel, crazy life

Is to discover your love

Your unique constellation

Your way of relating in the world

Your mission

Is to locate your web of light

Your pattern of connection

Your heart

In a universe of vast emptiness.

## Giving Up

I'm giving up –

Not on life, but on those actions that threaten
life

Not on living, but on those habits that distract
from living

Not on loving, but on those fears that get in the
way of loving

I'm giving up

Food that forges a chain of suffering and death

Clothes that weave a garment of exploitation
and shame

Fuels that are harbingers of cancer and climate
catastrophe

I'm giving up –

Not on people, but on the poor choices that people make

Not on freedom, but on the complacency that cripples freedom

Not on hope, but on the sense of impotence that kills all hope

I'm giving up

Words that break down rather than build others up

Work that lacks a larger purpose of improving society

Products that leave a trail of misery and waste in their wake

I'm giving up –

For the good of myself and those who have less
than I do

For the good of the planet and those who share
its blue-green bounty

For the good of the children and those who will
inherent what we leave behind


I'm giving up

All these things and more –

In my best and brightest and bravest moments
–

For good.

## Earth Spirit

Whenever life gets me down

When I feel disconsolate, disillusioned, disconnected

Wandering aimlessly and wondering wistfully

When something's amiss and I don't know what it is

I find it helps to call upon the spirit of the Earth

To invoke that which moves and breathes and infuses all life

To remind me of my vital place in the universe

Where I am inextricably linked, connected, enmeshed

Swaying in sync with the moon and tides

Stretching for the skies along with trees and birds

Singing in unconscious harmony with nature's chorus

And never truly alone, or cut off or superfluous

Never really without direction or bereft of love

For the great Earth Spirit enfolds me and entwines us

It binds our actions and amplifies our intentions

It is the spirit of possibility and positivity

The source of our energy and the web of our dreams

It bathes us in the wisdom of countless aeons

And heals us with the gentle rays of time

Therefore, in our hour of need and season of doubt

Let us be open to the promise of the Earth Spirit

To the hope that rises within us

To the faith that extends beyond us

To the love that gathers around us

Let us welcome the invisible power of the
   planet

And the indivisible power of the people

Let us be guardians and advocates of our Earth

Even as the Earth nurtures and cares for us

Let our Earth Spirit invocation be a
   commitment

To live and love in the highest and truest way
   we know

For the sake of ourselves

For the future of our children

And for the life of our only home, Earth.

## The Elements

When leaves are red and clouds are grey
When vision fades and edges fray
I turn towards the changing sky
To teach me that all things must die

When days are dark and nights are long
When less is more and right feels wrong
I call upon the patient earth
To teach me in the ways of birth

When branches bud and flowers bloom
When life emerges from the womb
I give my thanks for flowing streams
To teach me how to nurture dreams

When skies are blue and hopes are high
When love is bright and wishes fly
I turn towards the blazing sun
To teach me how the race is run

The elements of life's desire –
Air and water, earth and fire –
Combine to make the circle whole:
The swirl of body, mind and soul.

**Yes!**

I'm saying 'Yes!' to life
With all its cravings and curve-balls
With its delights and detours
Over rocky ground and smooth
Trusting the flow and determined
To enjoy the ride

I'm saying 'Yes!' to love
With all its beauty and blood-thorns
With its dope and disappointments
Over lovers lost and found
Trusting the wind and willing
To sail the seas

I'm saying 'Yes!' to learning
With all its flavours and false starts
With its secrets and surprises
Over letting go and giving
Trusting the path and open
To walk the bend

I'm saying 'Yes!' to living
With all its weirdness and wisdom
With its breakdowns and bust-ups
Over matters great and small
Trusting the light and happy
To share the shine.

## Earth Affirmation

I am the rock
Solid and silent
Watching the wheeling stars above me
Forming and transforming the landscape
With millennial patience

I am the tree
Standing and swaying
Sheltering the bustling life below me
Greening and redreaming the desert
With emergent vision

I am the river
Freeform and flowing
Quenching the thirsty needs around me
Snaking and remaking the valleys
With gentle artistry

I am the flower
Budding and blooming
Inviting the buzzing bees to kiss me
Lighting and brightening the meadows
With fragrant palette

I am the mountain
Sturdy and stretching
Touching the vaulted sky above me
Aspiring and inspiring the climbers
With panoramic promise

I am the forest
Dappled and diverse
Clothing the naked land beneath me
Breathing and reweaving the pattern
With tangled beauty

I am the ocean
Tugging and teasing
Courting the silver moon beyond me
Swelling and retelling the stories
With timeless mystery

I am the Earth
Vital and vulnerable
Defying the barren space around me
Thriving and surviving the fever
With resilient wisdom.

**The Valley of Doubt**

Should you find yourself
In the shadowed valley of doubt
Resist the glib temptation
To climb the first path you encounter
Rather linger in that unlit depth
Where new possibilities are gestating
Like a seed in the dark fecund earth

Should you catch yourself
On the swaying bridge of indecision
Let go the impulsive need
To move back to solid ground safety
Rather straddle that great divide
Where the tension of apparent opposites
May reveal a transcendent third way

Should you lose yourself
In the swirling mists of uncertainty
Fight back the compelling urge
To search blindly for the horizon
Rather be still amidst the chaos
Where seemingly random forces
Are connecting butterflies and typhoons

And as you wait, as you watch and wish
Be ever vigilant, be alert and alive
For when the right path appears
When the third way unveils itself
When synchronicity sparks brightly
You must rise and choose and act
With new hope, bold faith and brave love.

## To Lead

To lead or not to lead?
That is the wrong question
For in our hour of need
It's what to lead that matters more
The core of values and their strength
The door of possibilities
The planted seeds and fruits they bear
It's there true leadership resides
For tides are changing quickly now
It's not the who, it's where and how

Leaders come and leaders go
But which will show a better way
A brighter day because they led
A lighter tread upon the Earth
The birth of purpose in our lives
And work in which our spirit thrives
Let's not ignore the children's voice
The choice is ours, to lag or lead
To make the world more green and fair
In ways that care, that hope and dare

Don't tell me that you lead, for I
Will never be impressed
It's how you lead that interests me
And what you strive for without rest
It's where your dreams are taking us
And who will thrive the best
It's why you lead that tells me more
Than all the feathers in your nest
To lead is nothing special, for
To serve's the real test

To lead or not to lead?

The question's quite absurd

For leadership's the path that freed

The slaves and we need so much more

From shore to shore, where chains remain

And oceans rise, yet leaders' lies

Support charades and barricades

That cling to glories of the past

Rise up new leaders who can shape

A future that is built to last.

## Acting Now

I'm acting now – for the future
For all the children and their children
For the powerless and the voiceless
Because the time for talking is over
And the time for action is now

I'm acting now – for the planet
For all species and their habitats
For the web of life that is fraying
Because the time for excuses is over
And the time for action is now

I'm acting now – for the present
For all leaders and their followers
For the fearful and the hopeless
Because the time for delaying is over
And the time for action is now.

## It Matters

It matters that we live our life
And that we try and fail
But in the end what matters most
Is that we've told our tale

It matters that we learn to love
And that we win and lose
But in the end what matters most
Is that we've worn our shoes

It matters that we make our mark
And that we stretch and strive
But in the end what matters most
Is that we've been alive.

## Complexity

We're moving through the tangled maze
Connecting and reflecting
We're weaving on our loom of days
Creating and remaking

The map is never true nor clear
The path is never straight
And yet a pattern will appear
For we who watch and wait

We're surfing on the waves of change
Trusting and adjusting
We're dancing through the halls of strange
Twirling and unfurling

The music beat can always shift
The tides will ebb and flow
And yet a movement will emerge
To take us where we need to go.

## Futures Bright

Days may be dark and nights be long
But soon the song will change its tune
The beat will heat the winter's chill
Until the thrill returns to spark
And mark a sunrise, flaming red
To quench a hunger still unfed, a light
That's set to reignite the flight
Of dreams and schemes and imaginings.

Work may be hard and stress be high
But soon the sky will change its mood
The blaze of rays will melt the clouds
Until the shrouds are memories
Upon the breeze, the blue beyond
Like ripples on a tranquil pond, a sign
Across the arc of time to rhyme
Of scars and stars and destinies.

Life may be large and love be wide
But soon the tide will change its sway
The day you make your way towards
A cause that's calling out to you
To shift and shape, to reawake
The passion that's inside, the need
To grow and lead, the seed
Of traits and fates and futures bright.

## Garden Wise

I'm learning how to plant new seeds
To nurture sprouts and let them rise
I'm pruning back and pulling weeds
As branches sway to gentle sighs

I'm listening to the songs of birds
And watching bees and butterflies
I'm reading nature's book of words
As seasons turn, all lives and dies

I'm resting during winter's calm
And blooming with the springtime flowers
I'm soaking summer's healing balm
And letting go for autumn's hours

I'm finding secrets, tracing flows
And keeping faith while cutting ties
I'm conscious how my spirit grows
I'm slowly getting garden wise.

## Leap of Faith

You stood at the edge and took a deep breath
A leap of faith towards a future unknown
And with that leap, you died a small death
Like an old skin shed and a new one regrown

There's no need for fear, a leap's just a step
Made with firm resolve and noble intention
It's striding out with new vigour and pep
On a path full of hope and reinvention

Faith is believing before you can see
Following the trail with no summit in view
Knowing the acorn contains an oak tree
Finding your spirit and keeping it true

You stood at the edge and took that great leap

Now life will conspire to show you the way

And the lessons you learn, the dreams you will
reap

Are rewards for the actions you take every day.

## Regeneration

The news is good (have you not heard?)
For every insect, beast and bird
The Great Extinction's turning 'round
The seeds of change found fertile ground

The barren fields are set to bloom
The rivers sparkling crystal clear
New forests rise up from the gloom
The wild calls out for all to hear

The colour's back in coral reefs
We heed the words of tribal chiefs
The farms are making healthy soil
The sun and wind's replacing oil

The news is good (don't you agree?)
Nature's back, it's not too late
Across the land, the air and sea
We let the Earth regenerate.

## In the Mind

When this great race of life is run
When all is said and all is done
When we look back, we'll surely find
So much of life was in the mind

The hardest trials, the stress and strain
The darkest nights, the clouds and rain
The loss that left us bruised and blind
These were the battles of the mind

The proudest wins, the joy and fun
The brightest days, the skies and sun
The love that made us good and kind
These were the triumphs of the mind

When this great wheel of life is turned
When seasons pass and tides have churned
When we reflect on what's behind
We'll know it's true: life's in the mind.

## A Better Place

We may not sail the Seven Seas
Or board a rocket ship to Mars
Yet still we know to catch the breeze
And set our sights upon the stars

We may not run an enterprise
Or lead a nation and its realm
Yet still we have the wings to rise
And many ways to take the helm

We may not walk the halls of fame
Or take the prize in fortune's race
Yet still we stand behind our name
And make the world a better place.

## Because I Care

When I strike on the streets in mass protest
And warn you to change or beware
It's not because I'm foolhardy –
It's because I care
When I brood in the quagmire of worry
And greet your bright smile with a stare
It's not because I'm unhappy –
It's because I care

I care that the forests are burning
That the storms are grey prophets of gloom
I care that the children are yearning
For a future where nature can bloom

When I speak with the words of the voiceless

And lay my stark message out bare

It's not because I'm emotive –

It's because I care

When I spark with the flames of great passion

And hope that you'll take up my dare

It's not because I'm hot-headed –

It's because I care


I care that the homeless are growing

That the poor cannot flee from their pains

I care that the blood is still flowing

That the slaves are not free from their chains

When I strive for a future that's better
And look for a purpose to share
It's not because I'm a hippie –
It's because I care
When I burst with ideas for solutions
And tackle tough problems with flair
It's not because I'm creative –
It's because I care

I care that the animals suffer
That the farms are like factories of doom
I care that survival gets tougher
That the sixth mass extinction now looms

When I call for bold action on climate
And demand that you clean up the air
It's not because I'm dramatic –
It's because I care
When I speak of the need for more justice
And implore you to do what is fair
It's not because I'm a dreamer –
It's because I care

I care that all black lives should matter
That the scourge of race-hatred remains
I care that the women get battered
That they still have to fight for their gains

When I wish for rewilding of nature
And the right to protect life so rare
It's not because I'm a "greenie" –
It's because I care
When I join in the movement for changes
It's not my intention to scare
It's just me shaping our future –
It's because I care.

**It's Time**

It's time to redesign, to reconceive the world we
   leave

For those who follow in our wake, for each
   child's sake

It's time to spark and innovate, to syncopate
   with

New ideas, beyond the fears of failures past, at
   last

It's time to rise, with fire burning in our eyes

And change our ways to giving, for life and for
   the living

It's time to re-align, to reassess the mess we
make

When what we take is more than need, is greed

It's time to halt life's slow decline, the heinous
crime

Of ecocide, the plastic tide, the skies of smoke
that choke

It's time to heal the dying soil, to ease the
workers' toil

And make new waves of daring, with love and
with great caring

It's time to redefine, to resurrect the hope that springs

With wings of acting boldly now, with minds that beam

It's time to dream of futures green, to reinvent our fate

To help the Earth regenerate, where waste is food, renewed

It's time to turn from death, to take a breath, start afresh

And make a mighty pivot, for life and all who live it.

## A Swirling Story

Don't ever underestimate
The power of stories small and great
For tales of fairies, kings and queens
Are echoes of our human dreams

The way we live, the brands we choose
Are mirrors of our inner muse
They tell us who we'd like to be
Behind our masked identity

We'd sooner dance than tick and tock
We'd rather sing than punch a clock
For we're not made of cog and wheel
But minds that flash and hearts that feel

The way we work, the things we buy
Are answers to the question why
They draw a map to hidden gold
To buried fears and wishes bold

We'd sooner hear a myth or rhyme
We'd rather watch a film sublime
For we're not digits writ in code
But lilting lines within an ode

Each battling hero on a quest
Beseeches us to do our best
Each star-crossed lover's tender kiss
Evokes the call to find our bliss

Your life's a yarn that you must spin
With woven plots, you lose and win
Each tale's a spark that fuels the fire
A swirling story to inspire.

## Slow Time

We're marching in slow time
In nowhere to go time
And it's melting the clock
To a languid tick tock
The rhythm feels wrong
As time slithers and stretches
Every moment it etches
Takes ever so long

We're dreaming in no time
In no chance to flow time
And it's come to a stop
With a listless drip drop
The wisp of a song
Keeps time sliding and shuffling
Every heartbeat it's muffling
Still sounds like a gong

We're waking to show time

To ready to crow time

And it's picking up pace

For a thrills and spills race

The final furlong

Brings time speeding and stomping

Every step takes us romping

Back where we belong

## Connected

In life we form a complex web
Of patterns always shifting
We're tied to every other thing
No matter that we're drifting
We see ourselves in spangled skies
Of silver light reflected
We're twirling in a cosmic dance
Forever we're connected

Each day we add another thread
Of faith and hope entwining
A tapestry of weaves and knots
And love that's redefining
We see ourselves in healing cards
And totem poles erected
We're joining in an ancient song
That chants we're all connected

The river flows, the seasons sway
To moods of inner weather
With secret codes and hidden rhymes
In traces of a feather
We see ourselves in nature's glass
With energies affected
We're syncing global consciousness
We'll always be connected.

## Through Your Eyes

The world is different through your eyes

The shapes and angles, the colours and
    spangles

All sparring and jarring, shifting and
    shimmering

Making up a living mosaic, a patterned portrait

With each give and take, each grip and shake

You make something unique, something
    wonderful

Which I peek – each time you act or speak –

I see a better, brave world, through your eyes

The world is changing through your choices

The views and voices, the stands that you take

All the paths you make, with byways and
bridges

Making up a living map, a sculpted terrain

With more options to give, more chances to live

You make something renewed, something
hopeful

Like a potion brewed – each time you choose –

I see a brighter, bolder world, through your
choices

The world is growing through your knowing

The curious questions, the fresh discoveries

The bubbling and bursting, sizzling and thirsting

Making up a living book, a library of wisdom

With each word and idea, each step beyond fear

You make something meaningful, something that matters

With an impact that scatters, in each ripple

I see a wider, wiser world, through your knowing.

## Only Now

There's only now – this moment of this day
In time's great ocean, as we swell and sway
Between waves of memories already past
And hopeful dreams like fishnets cast

The day itself may change to foul or fair
Our only task is to be present there
To ride out the storm and soak up the sun
To manage the fear and relish the fun

There's only now – this fleeting time and place
In life's long journey, the truth we must face
Is that though the ground we cover is great
The path that we tread is what we create

The place itself may bring pleasure or pain
Sometimes we will lose, sometimes we will gain
The trick's to be present through thick and thin
For life's not a race, there's nothing to win

There's only now – this breath in, this breath out

A state of being is what it's about

To be here right now, to be who we are

To beat like a drum, to shine like a star.

## Think on Business

You may think on business and despair
See it's ugly face of greed laid bare
How it chokes the seas and fouls the air
And the workers' lot is never fair

But there's another story being told
Of a smarter way and leaders bold
Of fresh purpose starting to unfold
And business breaking from the mould

It's a tale of seeing with new eyes
And of commerce learning to be wise
Where there's innovation on the rise
And trust beyond what money buys

For when business cares it regenerates
And changes what it risks and rates
It begins to give more than it takes
And reinvents the world it makes

When nature thrives and people grow
Returns for business start to flow
As those who reinvest will know
The future reaps the seeds we sow

You may think on business and take heart
For a better way is ours to chart
We all have our roles, we play our part
But there's no time to lose, so make a start.

## Thriving

Our life is so much more than a duty or a chore
Of merely getting by without a why or what for
The law of tooth and claw, the struggle to exist
To rally and resist against life's slow decay
The way of entropy, of living just to see
Another day, to stay, to endure and survive
No, life is meant to thrive

In nature all things grow, from seed to tree, we know

The cycle of living through giving, of reap and sow

The flow, things come and go, the cycles of grooming

From sprouting to blooming, of stretching for the light

The bright palette of hope, the diverse ways to cope

To cherish and flourish, bursting forth and alive

For nature means to thrive

Society lives too, a melting pot we brew

From cultures and crises, with spices for flavour

And kindness to savour, ideas for conceiving

And goals for achieving that stretch us and bind us

That find us, together in all kinds of weather

Wanting what's fair, to care, longing to love and strive

For society to thrive

The markets live and breathe in complex webs
we weave

The synapses of trade have made the things we
need

Each deed a chance to lead, while tech is
getting smart

Yet still, it needs a heart, a compass as a guide

To tide us through the storm and find a better
norm

A breakthrough to renew, an innovation drive

Yes, markets too can thrive

All life is meant to rise, to reach up to the skies

To move beyond the edge, to fledge with
hopeful cries

Life tries until it flies, it shakes and spreads its
wings

And trills each note it sings, while given time
and space

The race of life is run, full powered by the sun

On land, in seas, like bees' sweet nectar from
the hive

All life is made to thrive.

## A Place to Thrive

Is the world a better place
Because we lived and loved and learned?
What will our children have to face
Because of what we built and burned?

Are people better than before
Because we gave them dignity?
What happened to the sick and poor
While we were living strong and free?

Is the world a fairer place
Because we fought for equal rights?
Who lost for us to win our race
Or did we open up new heights?

Is nature thriving great and small
Because we walked upon the earth?
Did oceans rise and species fall
With every breath we took since birth?

Is the world a dying place
Because our enterprises grew?
Did we destroy our living space
Or did we seed the world anew?

Each day we get to use our voice
To raise the tide or let it ebb
Each day we face a simple choice
To nurture life or fray its web

Let's let the world be better still
For every moment we're alive
Because we choose to use our will
To make our earth a place to thrive.

## If

If you can believe in yourself
When others doubt you
If you can conceive of solutions
Where others see problems
If you can relieve life's stresses
While others get stuck
Then you will achieve your ambitions
On your own terms

If you can define your purpose
To answer the "why"
If you can align your knowledge
To fill in the "what"
If you can refine your skill-set
To strengthen the "how"
Then you will design your career
To serve your needs

If you can survive each crisis

And learn from it

If you can revive each failure

And start again

If you are alive to each moment

And take your chances

Then you will thrive in each facet

Of work, love and life.

## Never Too Late

It's never too dark to light with a spark
The blackness of night as colours flash bright
To flame in the gloom and leave a good mark
There's always a gleam of hope left in sight
It's never too dark, not ever too dark

It's never too bold to break from the mould
Of habits and rules, of nations and schools
To rewrite the plot of tales we've been told
There's always a magus dressed as a fool
It's never too bold , not ever too bold

It's never too soon to shoot for the moon
With visions and schemes, with rockets and
  dreams
To wish on a star, go bust and then boom
There's always a chance to catch the sunbeams
It's never too soon, not ever too soon

It's never too high to reach for the sky
With ladders to climb, one step at a time
To strive without rest, to fail and retry
There's always a rhythm, always a rhyme
It's never too high, not ever to high

It's never too late to regenerate
Our land and our seas, the fish and the trees
To rewild the earth and change the world's fate
There's always new life buzz-buzzing like bees
It's never too late, not ever too late

## Healers of the Earth

Some may see a patch of dirt
But you see so much more
You see a place where seeds can grow
Where nature can restore
The living soil, the buds of hope
The blooms and buzzing bees
You see a place of flourishing
Of birds and frogs and trees
For we are healers of the Earth
We make her frayed web whole
And as we do, we heal ourselves
In body, mind and soul.

## The Stoic

I am a stoic
But that does not mean
That I deny life's pleasures
Rather, I embrace the fullness of life
Always delighted by its highs
And ever expecting its lows
Knowing that the path to equanimity
Lies somewhere in between

I am a stoic
But that does not mean
That I dull down life's colours
Rather, I accept the vagaries of life
Always influencing what I can
And letting go of the rest
Knowing that the secret to happiness
Is telling the difference

I am a stoic
But that does not mean
That I spurn life's potential
Rather, I study the patterns of life
Always finding beauty everywhere
And befriending the chaos
Knowing that the purpose of existence
Is to have existed at all.

## Nature Speaks

Our days are filled with vexing noise
Of chatter that doesn't matter
Of news that makes us lose our poise
A cacophony of clatter
Yet underneath the fuzz and buzz
Listen for a pitter patter
Of tiny feet or falling rain
Of eyes that blink and batter

For nature speaks in dulcet tones
In whispered sighs upon the breeze
In songs that echo in our bones
And secrets swirling through the seas
She speaks in tacit clues and codes
For nature likes to taunt and tease
She speaks with pulsing fungal webs
Through elephants and trees

Our days are filled with chance and choice

With sounds of seasons passing by

And every moment has a voice

A susurration or a cry

For nature speaks with endless tongues

That teach us how to fail and fly

Each lesson holds a vital kōan

For how we live our life and why.

**Call to Adventure**

This is a call to adventure:

To set off together for distant lands

To stand with each other through shifting
sands

Trusting the current enough to let go

Having the wisdom to go with the flow


Adventures are invitations:

To see the world through different eyes

To try and fail, to see what flies

Knowing the map is never true

Reading the signs, chasing the blue


This is a call to adventure:

To puzzle together through every maze

To learn from each other for all your days

Growing by living, like birds on the wing

Changing through seasons from winter to
spring

Adventures are journeys:
To fill the heart and stretch the mind
To lose the way, to seek and find
Reading the stars, the sun and moon
Happy in sync, whistling a tune

This is a call to adventure:
To stay strong together through storm and sun
To fight for each other and stand as one
Trusting the pathway and where it will lead
Having the patience to nurture love's seed

## Enigma

Your life is a giant puzzle
A maze of mystery and secrets
But what are you searching for?
What is the code that needs cracking
At the heart of life's enigma?

It's about finding out what you like
And working hard to ensure
That it becomes what you're good at
Because life's too short and difficult
To be doing what you don't like

It's about finding out who you love
And taking care to ensure
That they remain your main priority
Because life's too long and incredible
To be with anyone you don't love

It's about finding out who you are
And taking steps to ensure
That you love that person unconditionally
Because life's too strange and precious
To be chasing someone else's shadow

Your life is an epic expedition
A trail of valleys and summits
And what you are moving towards
What you are discovering along the way
Is an answer to life's question.

## On the Brink

It's true, our world is on the brink
A species gone each time we blink
Each one another broken link
As oceans rise and nations sink

So much is lost, so much to mourn
So high the cost, so deep the scorn
Yet something new is being born
The blackest night precedes the dawn

Our time is short, we're in a race
We must act now, pick up the pace
The simple truth we all must face
Is nature needs to take back space

Let's let new life reseed and grow
Let woods come back and rivers flow
Rewild the land and seas and know
That nature thrives when we let go.

## The Race of Our Lives

We are in the race of our lives

Whether or not we know it, running slow or
fast

While time, our enduring opponent

Is patient, plodding, turning the future into the
past


And we, like the hare of our folktales

Dart hither and thither, diverted and delighted

Rushing from moment to fleeting moment

Beyond the narrow track, the finish line
unsighted


We are in the race of our lives

Though we may linger, and languish, and
squander

As if we have all the breath in the world

And it matters not how we live and where we
wander

For we, unlike the tortoise of our sun's daily
march

Mistake speed for progress, and miles for
meaning

Chasing each mirage, be it gain or glory or love

Straying from the course, distracted by our
dreaming

We are in the race of our lives

Yet in the final strait, who cares how or where
we ran

It matters only that we took part at all, and in
the end

That we know ourselves better than when we
began.

**Travel Far**

As you travel far and venture wide

Expect the tide to ebb and flow, the ride

Of life won't always go the way you want

And though you may not know the reasons
why

Yet still you must try, and fail and try again

For when you learn to rise and fall

To compromise your dreams and go on
dreaming

You will find that life rewards you

In unexpected ways, on days when you are
down

When the road is tough and you've had enough
You will win, because life's just like that
It's fickle, when it's not a flood it's a trickle
And you must navigate the twists and turns
The chills and burns, and the longer you do
The stronger you get, you let life teach you
As you learn to be lost and follow your star
As you venture wide and travel far.

## And We Grow

Life is full of twists and turns
So many things we cannot know
Yet step by step we make our way
And as we do, we learn and grow

We may have lines upon our face
We may have scars and stars to show
Yet day by day we tell our tale
And as we do, our stories grow

Love is full of joy and pain
As seasons turn and rivers flow
Yet hand in hand we venture forth
And as we do, we shine and grow.

## We Have Earth

Who needs heaven when we have skies
That blush and bruise in pinks and blues
That puff and swish to eagles' cries
Who needs heaven when we have eyes

Who needs wishing when we have trees
That stretch and sway in green and grey
That creak and kiss like living seas
Who needs wishing when we have bees

Who needs dreaming when we have earth
That seeds and blooms in fragrant tunes
That conjures life from dark and dearth
Who needs dreaming when we have rebirth

## A Butterfly Appeared

Yesterday, a butterfly appeared

Fluttering at my windowpane, trapped on the
inside,

Trying to get out, flummoxed, no matter how it
tried,

By the invisible wall, the air of glass – and I
feared

That all that's right and all that's wrong with
the world

Was wrapped up in that moment, tightly furled:

A vision of light, as all the while, darkness
neared.

For here was beauty, nature at its most
    sublime

Within my grasp, though I had no thought of
    grasping,

A sign of something fleeting, yet strangely
    everlasting

As if capturing the mystery and paradox of time

For a butterfly – that quintessential symbol of
    change –

Is now at odds with the world we carelessly
    rearrange

To suit our rhythm and reason, without rhyme

We, the standing ape, who in our great escape

From the trees and from all things wild,
    untamed,

Have made a home for ourselves and proudly
    claimed

That what we choose to overuse is not rape,

Only dominion – in truth, domination – over all

Until, in our arrogance, life itself begins to stall,

An age of extinction, an earth bent out of
    shape.

Do I read too deep? Was it just a random
    butterfly?

Of course, I opened the window and let it out,

A small victory for life and freedom; no doubt

An insignificant act, yet it felt good, at least to
    try,

Yet later that day, another butterfly was
    trapped

And I released it too, and a third and fourth
    appeared, flapped

And flailed, a tap-tap dance of panic on the
    glassy sky.

And so, it seems that my help was a delusion –

Quick fixes always are – for it did not touch the cause,

The root of the problem, the artificial laws

That keep us wanting more, the unnatural profusion

Of things that we don't need, that do not nourish

Our spirits, or allow nature's great web to flourish

And so, we continue, blissful in our confusion.

Still, this is the moment to change, as the end
nears,

For endings can be beginnings, if we let go,

If we give up crawling and take to flying, we
grow,

For we are not prisoners of our darkest fears,

We can act to reseed the earth and rewild the
sea,

We can choose to free up space for all life to be,

For the next butterfly that appears.

## The Great Outdoors

I always pause when "love of the great
    outdoors" is invoked,

For it raises awkward questions, and I find I
    am provoked –

Not to question the sincerity of any love that's
    so confessed,

Nor the greatness of what lies beyond – we can
    but be impressed,

For doors are potent portals, thresholds of the
    in-between

That join two worlds, that draw a veil over
    mysteries unseen.

Why do I pause and ponder each time I hear
  that phrase?

It's because of what it stands for, and the
  mindset it betrays,

For when we say "the great outdoors", we really
  mean to say

That nature, wild and beautiful, is "out there",
  far away,

As if our lives were separate, a world apart, a
  life inside

And nature stands opposed, beyond ourselves,
  the chasm wide.

No wonder, then, that we ignore, neglect,
  exploit, abuse,

For nature is objectified, she's there for us to
  use,

And so, we grub and grope and grab, and pay
  with tips of waste;

At best, we find her pleasure zones, then leave
  again in haste.

It seems to me a sordid tale of domination,
  master-slave,

In which we feed our appetites, try to possess
  what we so crave.

'That's just not true!' I hear you cry, 'It's not
like that at all,

We love our nature, fair and green, we're ever
in its thrall.

We visit her great wilderness, we even pick our
trash;

Your accusations are a lie, your arguments are
rash!

And even in the city, you'll often find us in the
park

(Although it's not a place to be alone and after
dark)'.

I hear your plea, I empathise, I feel that way
    myself sometimes,

And yet the way you speak of nature clearly
    underlines

How separate you have become, how dumb and
    deaf and blind,

For you and nature are the same, with
    destinies entwined.

There is no door between us, no gap to step
    beyond,

For nature is our only home, a living web, our
    family bond.

So, when next someone you know invokes "the
    great outdoors",

Reflect on what they mean and if you share
    their subtle cause,

For nature's no more outdoors than nature's in
    our homes

And in our hearts, our minds and blood, and in
    our very bones;

Nature is the loom of life, the warp and weft
    with which we weave

And every thread we cut or mend affects the
    legacy we leave.

I love that you love nature, which simply
  means you love yourself,

But nature's not an elixir, a tonic for your
  mental health;

It's every living thing on earth, and how we are
  connected;

It's the microbe and the Milky Way as images
  reflected;

It's great for sure, both out and in and every
  way you see it,

For nature's us and we are nature – we only
  need to be it.

**Letter to Earth**

Dear Earth

I have some things I'd like to say, things I need
    to get off my chest,

But feelings can be tricky, so I thought that
    pen and paper's best.

I'm writing you this letter, to explain myself, as
    best I can,

And, not to spoil the surprise, but I'm just
    about your biggest fan.

*Part 1. I See You*

If you were our mother, I wonder, would you be
proud or sad?

Would you see our kindness, the good in our
hearts, and be glad?

Would you rejoice in what we've achieved, the
lessons that we've learned?

And what of the chances we've squandered, the
bridges that we've burned?


I want to say: I see you!

Though, in truth, at times I close my eyes

For what we humans do sometimes makes me
quite ashamed

We have inflicted our ugliness, peddled our lies

I only hope that what's been lost still can be
regained

I see your beauty, and how you have been
  scarred

Your jungles cut, your mountains mined, your
  grasslands charred

I see your bounty, and how you have been
  scammed

Your creatures killed, your airways choked,
  your rivers jammed


I want to say: I see you!

Your emerald forests and umber sands

Your sapphire oceans and azure skies

Your mountain peaks and frozen lands

Your coves and caves where mystery lies

*Part 2. I Hear You*

If you were our father, I wonder, would you be
    calm or mad?

Would you cherish our resilience, stand by our
    actions, good and bad?

Would you relish the battles we've fought, no
    matter if we lost or won?

And what of the havoc we've unleashed, the
    destruction that we've spun?


I want to say: I hear you!

Though, in truth, at times I block my ears

For what we people do sometimes leaves me
    quite disturbed

We have amplified our noisiness, trumpeted
    our fears

I only hope that what's been hushed can one
    day be reheard

I hear your melody, and how you have been muted

Your chorus stifled, your voice muffled, your wisdom refuted

I hear your symphony, and how it turns to silence

Your songs distorted, your cries ignored, your peace met with violence


I want to say: I hear you!

Your singing whales and tweeting birds

Your shrieking storms and sighing breeze

Your howling wolves and grunting herds

Your roaring lions and creaking trees

*Part 3. I'm Sorry*

If you were our child, I wonder, would you be
    happy or furious?

Would you look forward to your future with
    bright unbridled hope?

Would you be carefree, would you play, would
    you be curious?

And would you understand our folly when
    you're struggling to cope?


I want to say: I'm sorry!

Though, in truth, at times I seal my lips

For what our leaders do sometimes, I have to
    say, I hate it

We have taken your wild places and turned
    them into tips

I only hope that what's been spoiled can be
    rejuvenated

I feel your disappointment and how you've been
neglected

Your land poisoned, your seas polluted, your
biodiversity affected

I feel your melancholy and how you've been
degraded

Your wetlands drained, your corals bleached,
your living treasures raided

I want to say: I'm sorry!

For being so careless with your gift of life

For being so selfish with my unquenchable
need

For being so childish with my endless strife

For being so callous with my insatiable greed

*Part 4. I Love You*

If you were our deity, I wonder, would you be
   angry or forgiving?

Would you give us another chance; another
   chance at living?

Would you want us to carry on, or rather wipe
   the slate all clear?

And would you be willing to help us, teach us;
   would you hold us dear?


I want to say: I love you!

Though, in truth, at times I harden my heart

For what we humans do sometimes makes us
   undeserving

We've cut so many sacred strands and torn
   your web apart

I only hope we'll realise your life is worth
   preserving

I love your wholeness, and how you manage to
    survive

Your vitality, your diversity, your myriad ways
    to thrive

I love your openness, and how you reach up for
    the skies

Your buds in spring, your blooming flowers,
    your elusive butterflies


I want to say: I love you!

Your kaleidoscope of colours, your infinity of
    shapes

Your secrets of the helix code and evolution's
    tree

Your everchanging seasons, the patterns
    weather makes

Your puzzle of creation, and maze paths to be
    free

*P.S.*

I had these things to say, so I've written you
    this letter

Though now I realise, I wrote it more for me
    than you

I wrote to say how much I care, and that I'll do
    much better

And if I'm not mistaken, I think that maybe you
    care too

Lots of love

Your Great Admirer.

## Let It Begin

I'm thinking it's not too late, that our fate is not
sealed,

That the race of life is far from run; we're not
done,

For we wield the wand of choice, we have a
voice,

We can speak for the Earth, and not let her
perish,

Take care of her creatures and all that we
cherish,

For we're not ready to give up, or stand idly by

And watch our mother die.


Let it begin, with protecting more, then let's
restore

The land and sea, let's win back what we've
lost,

Before the cost becomes too high, because the
sky's

The limit and fortune favours those who try.

I'm dreaming of a new world, of nature
   unfurled

In swirls of blue and curls of green, in bursts of
   yellow

And swathes of pink, each time I blink another
   species

Comes back from the brink, another habitat is
   restored

To health, and the wealth of ecosystems
   returns,

Emerging from the gloom of the womb to give
   birth

To a revitalised Earth.


Let it begin, with the wolves and whales, as we
   tip the scales

Of trophic cascades, and as our fear fades we
   realise

That hunter and prey are performing a dance, a
   rhyme

That gives us a chance to reanimate the world,
   given time.

I'm learning that nature is resilient, that it's
    brilliant

At bouncing back, if only we give it space, the
    lack

Of bugs and birds, of fish and trees can be
    reversed

In a burst of recovery, as the great extinction
    turns

Into a great flourishing, a nourishing of roots
    and shoots,

As biota and biomes, cycles and food webs are
    repaired

And their bounty is shared.


Let it begin, with the factories and farms,
    turning harms

Into new ways of making and growing, of
    showing

How waste can be nutrients, and soils be alive,

For life coils like a spring, forever poised to
    thrive.

I'm turning dreams into action, and gaining traction

As solutions take hold and scale, as we dare to be bold

And fail, while tales of our success spreads, like bees

From flower to flower, the power is in our hands,

To clean up the oceans, and heal our lands,

And so I'm choosing to detox, to reseed and rewild,

For the hopes of a child.


Let it begin.

## Radical Activist

You call me a radical activist
Condemning my actions as touting extremes
No doubt there's a need for instruction
For it's high praise, if you know what it means

What else should I be, if not radical
For radical means to go back to the roots
A farmer begins by preparing the earth
And seeding the soil, in time, brings new
    shoots

You call me a radical activist
For sourcing the problem or ultimate cause
No doubt it results in disruption
Or blocking and breaking unjustified laws

And what else should I be, if not active
(I'll be passive enough when I'm done and dead)
The world needs a shake-up to wake it
And the legacy ways, like leaves, must be shed

You call me a radical activist

And I thank you kindly for this accolade

No doubt it's the path of construction

Of shaping and shifting – our future remade.

## I Like to Move It

Nothing comes to those who stand still
For life is a dance of changes
A puzzle that rearranges
Shaped by the power of our will

It's not that we are in control
Or that we reach our every dream
Still we must paddle in the stream
If we're to move towards our goal

That means we have to take a chance
And trust that we can make it work
There is no time to slack or shirk
Or give our fears a second glance

This is true, though I can't prove it
Stand still long enough and you're dead
For as a wise lemur once said:
"I like to move it, move it!"

## Right Action, Right Mind

The older I get, the more I find
That I am gentle with myself; not blind
To my mistakes, but more forgiving,
More wise about the purpose of living

For life is not a race to win or lose
It's more about walking in our own shoes
And it's not an exam to pass or fail
It's more about weaving our unique tale

The older I get, the more I see
That changing the world starts inside of me
For life invites us to care, to be kind
As the Buddha says: right action, right mind.

## Change the World

*Part 2*

Let's change the world, let's move it
Let's chance it and free dance it
Let's feel its sliding rhythms
The echoes of its rhymes
The calling of our times
With signs of stars aligning
With mimes of joy and madness
Of syncopated sadness
Because we bend, because we tend
To lose the beat, then find it
To live life forward, not rewind it
Let's stamp our feet, link arms and say:
We'll change the world today!

Let's change the world, invoke it

Let's weave it and conceive it

Let's sing our songs of freedom

The myths of heroes' quests

The trial-by-fire tests

With rests to ease our struggle

With crests that draw us onward

Because we roam, because we've shown

With tears and wide-eyed wonder

These days are not for squander

Let's choose our narrative to say:

We changed the world today!

Let's change the world, let's heed it
Let's hear it and not fear it
Let's place our finger on life's pulse
Where mountain rivers flow
Where ancient forests grow
We know, for elders tell us
We grow by seeing what can be
Because within we find our jinn
And rub each deep desire
From sparks into bright flames of fire
Let's wish for every chance to say:
I changed the world today!

www.ingramcontent.com/pod-product-compliance
Lightning Source LLC
LaVergne TN
LVHW051240080426
835513LV00016B/1680